My Little Golden Book About
WEATHER

By Dennis R. Shealy
Illustrated by Xindi Yan

The editors would like to thank Elizabeth W. Mills, associate director of the American Meteorological Society Education Program, for her assistance in the preparation of this book.

A GOLDEN BOOK • NEW YORK

Text copyright © 2020 by Penguin Random House LLC
Cover art and interior illustrations copyright © 2020 by Xindi Yan
All rights reserved. Published in the United States by Golden Books, an imprint of Random House Children's Books, a division of Penguin Random House LLC, 1745 Broadway, New York, NY 10019. Golden Books, A Golden Book, A Little Golden Book, the G colophon, and the distinctive gold spine are registered trademarks of Penguin Random House LLC.
rhcbooks.com
Educators and librarians, for a variety of teaching tools, visit us at RHTeachersLibrarians.com
Library of Congress Control Number: 2019930889
ISBN 978-0-593-12323-2 (trade) — ISBN 978-0-593-12324-9 (ebook)
Printed in the United States of America
10 9 8 7 6 5 4 3 2

Have you ever spent a sunny afternoon playing in the park when it suddenly started to rain? Or have you ever missed school because of a snowstorm? That's **weather**!

Weather can be cold or hot, dry or rainy, windy or calm. And weather can change from one type to another in the same day!

It all starts with the **sun**—and not just on sunny days! As Earth travels around the sun, the sun's energy helps determine our daily weather conditions as well as our yearly seasons.

Because our planet is rotating on a tilted axis, the area of Earth that is leaning toward the sun gets more heat and light. That creates a warm, sunny **summer** season on that part of the planet. The part that is tilted away from the sun experiences a cold and snowy **winter**. *Brrrr!*

Between summer and winter are two other seasons. Summer changes to **fall** in the areas where Earth begins to tilt away from the sun. These areas then get less light and warmth. The green leaves on the trees start to change to red, orange, yellow, and brown and fall to the ground.

Then things start to warm up as winter becomes **spring**. With more sunlight and warmth comes lots of rain. Trees sprout new leaves, and plants start growing.

Weather conditions such as rain and snow are part of the seasons, but how does the water get into the sky in the first place?

Again, the answer is the sun! The sun's heat makes the water in puddles, rivers, lakes, and oceans turn into water vapor, which is an invisible gas. Air containing the water vapor is heated by the sun and rises into the sky.

As the rising air cools, tiny water droplets form. These are **clouds**! Rain, sleet, hail, and snow fall from different types of clouds. This whole process is known as the **water cycle**. It's how water continually circulates all around the world!

Rain is simply the water returning to the ground in its liquid form. Rain can come in gentle showers or heavy downpours.

Rain makes plants grow and provides fresh water for drinking. It also makes puddles that are fun to jump in.

SPLASH!

Fog and **mist** happen when tiny water droplets stay close to the ground. They're like clouds that you can walk through! But be careful—fog and mist can make it difficult to see where you're going.

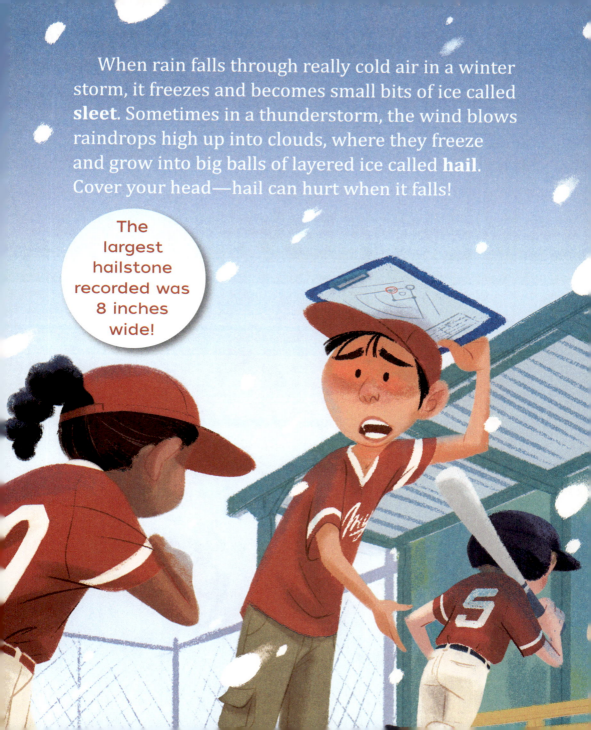

When rain falls through really cold air in a winter storm, it freezes and becomes small bits of ice called **sleet**. Sometimes in a thunderstorm, the wind blows raindrops high up into clouds, where they freeze and grow into big balls of layered ice called **hail**. Cover your head—hail can hurt when it falls!

The largest hailstone recorded was 8 inches wide!

Snow isn't formed by freezing water, like hail and sleet are. When conditions are right, fluffy ice crystals form in the clouds. They fall to Earth as snow—and if there's enough of it, you might get a day off from school! Yay!

Snow days are fun, but if too much snow falls, it can stop traffic, close airports, keep food from getting to grocery stores, and cause power lines to fall, which cuts off our electricity. This kind of storm—with heavy snow and strong winds—is called a **blizzard**.

No two snowflakes are exactly alike. Each one is unique—just like you!

Snowstorms and other types of weather create **wind**. That's what we call the air when it is moving. On a windy day, we can fly kites, enjoy the breeze, ride in sailboats, and even make electric power!

Wind is called a breeze, a gale, a storm, or a hurricane, depending on how powerful it is.

Hurricanes are huge spinning storms that form over the ocean. They can be 300 miles wide and generate heavy rain, powerful winds, and crashing waves. The calm area at the center of a hurricane is called the eye.

Hurricanes are also called cyclones or typhoons, depending on their location.

A hurricane has winds of 74 miles per hour or more.

During some kinds of storms, the air in the clouds may start to spin and form a giant funnel. If the funnel comes down to the ground, it's called a **tornado**.

Thunderstorms happen when clouds grow really large and dark. They will start to produce a lot of rain and wind. Large sparks of electricity called lightning flash in the sky.

Lightning can make a loud crashing sound called thunder.

KA-BOOM!

When you hear thunder, play indoors until the storm is over.

Don't worry about strong storms. Scientists called **meteorologists** keep track of all kinds of weather. They use tools as simple as a thermometer and as advanced as satellites to understand what's happening so they can make forecasts about what the weather will be like.

Forecasts help farmers figure out when to plant their crops, help airline pilots track the safest conditions for travel, and help everyone decide what to wear when they leave the house.

And that means *you* know when it'll be a great day to be outside!